AF610465

The Realistic Mental Aptitude

The Answer to your problems

The techniques that will help you achieve your objectives.

Javier almenar

Translation by Olga Núñez Miret

Cover art by Pili Vallejo.

Translation By Olga Núñez Miret

ISBN-13: 978-1-291-38880-0

1st Edition.

Printed in Spain

I dedicate this book to my grandparents who taught me many things and encouraged me on the long journey of life. I also dedicate this book to my daughters, who without their knowing helped me be strong in many difficult times. Finally, to my partner who has shown me what true LOVE between couples is.

TABLE OF CONTENTS

Prologue

The year 2012 is a complicated year, everybody talking about the crisis, unemployment, cuts, corrupt politicians, loss of workers' rights, loss of society's values, the meagre opportunities for the youth, the non-existent opportunities for adults, and so on. I could write a book by just enumerating what we already know and can't solve.

Evidently, this book is not claiming to give a solution to the global situation we are living in. We all know books that tell us how to solve our problems, how to better ourselves, how to change and improve our situation…in summary, how to change our lives.

This book does not aspire to any of that. You're not going to find here the magic wand to change everything that makes you unhappy, because such a formula does not exist. I don't want you to be searching for an answer to all your problems here, because by simply fact of living new situations and problems will arise. It's unavoidable. In conclusion, I don't want you to think that I'm going to give you the key to finding a job, to becoming rich, or to conquering the love of that person you dream of, or many other things you'll read about in the book.

The only intention of this book is to try and explain a series of guidelines and to apply a technique that will allow us to obtain the things we intend to do, to improve our life and obtain results in any field we choose.

I simply invite you to read this book and reach your own conclusions. I want you to get to the final page and weight up what you have learned or not from it, what you think, what has made it worth reading and what not, but more than anything what the book intends is to make you change the way you see and confront certain problems.

I'm sure I'm going to be subject to many criticisms from illustrious writers of books on self-development and self-help, from psychologists, and even from very well-informed people in these fields. They are going to say that I have no expertise to talk about such matters. Nothing further from the truth. I've been reading self-help books for over twenty years, and I'm not worried about such opinions, what I'm really concerned about is the conclusions you and many like you reach on reading it; people who can benefit from simple guidelines, easy to use but effective. The main ones you'll read about in the book, but others you'll discover yourselves in time by applying the relevant techniques.

All the guidelines I offer in the book, I have used them myself and can guarantee that they work.They are working for me and you'll see they are easy to follow.

I know that reading this book will help lots of people, when this happens, I will have achieved my goal.

I am fully convinced that you will gain something from reading this book. It is difficult to say in advance exactly what this might be, but when you reach the end of the book you'll find three blank pages. There you have to write the conclusions you have reached. You'll be surprised when you later read them. These few lines will be the guide you must follow. And then you will begin to value this book.

PART 1

The technique of the realistic mental aptitude

1. Positive or realistic mental aptitude.

What a dilemma! How many times have we heard it said that to change our situation we must have a positive mental aptitude? Evidently nobody is going to tell us that we should have a negative aptitude, and I'm not going to either.

Another interesting question is: What do you think of the realistic mental aptitude?

First we must know what "realistic" means. According to the Oxford Dictionary of English "realistic" is: having or showing a sensible and practical idea of what can be achieved or expected: *I thought we had a realistic chance of winning*.

Therefore what we need is to have a mental aptitude that allows us to act in a sensible and practical way to effect the changes we want to create in our life, trying to adjust ourselves and our goals to what can be achieved or expected.

Let's use an example. We have a small local football team (from the neighbourhood) that is going to play a match against one of the best four teams in the premiership. During the six months prior to the match we'll use a number of positive phrases to improve the mental aptitude ("we're going to win the match", "we are good enough to triumph", "there's no difference, eleven players against eleven, therefore we'll win").

We can also work on achieving a positive mental aptitude with the help of visual aids, for example we can pin a notice behind our bedroom door with the result we want to achieve, we can also stick a photo of our team lifting the trophy we're playing for (these days not difficult to do with digital photography programmes).

We have now created the basics to make our positive mental aptitude work for us every day for the six months prior to the match.

We could use many more techniques to reinforce our positive mental aptitude. How many times have we been told that repetition can help us achieve our objective; in this case we would repeat thousands of times the phrase: "we're going to win this match". O we could always use the well know phrase: "Yes, we can".

Honestly, do you think the team has any possibility of wining the match? No, of course not, the probability is non-existent. Then, what failed? During six months we've been using techniques that have created a positive mental aptitude but in spite of all that we lost the match. If we've done everything as suggested, what happened?

First, we'll be very disappointed because we haven't won the match, and second we'll begin to have doubts about the techniques used to achieve a positive aptitude.

Does this mean that the techniques are not useful to achieve a positive aptitude? Of course they're useful, but then, why didn't we achieve our goal that was wining the match? It's really simple; in the question itself lays the solution to the problem.We made a mistake when we chose the goal; we wanted to win the match, but that should not have been our objective, we should have been trying to achieve a different goal.But, how can I know which goal I should aim for?

The key resides in having a realistic mental aptitude, and according to it, we can define our goals.

In our example it's very easy to define the realistic mental aptitude; we must agree that for obvious reasons we cannot win the match, our team is a small neighbourhood team, our opponents are a professional team, full of players better than us. If we are clear about the true situation, we will be better able to define our goal, and therefore it will be easier for us to achieve it.

Let's think that our objective is to enjoy the match to the maximum, because we're going to play against admired footballers, because at the end of the match we'll be able to exchange T-shirts with our idols, because our families will see us surrounded by football stars on TV and the press, because our public will enjoy seeing our team and the opponents, and we could carry on listing a large number of objectives, and the least important one would be the final score.

All these objectives and many more will be easily achievable, for a simple reason, because we have a realistic mental aptitude. And if we reach our goals, what will we have achieved? Only happiness, well-being; we'll achieve a state of being that we have rarely attained, and all simply because we have analysed the situation from a realistic prism, with a realistic mental aptitude.

We don't need to choose between a positive mental aptitude and a realistic mental aptitude, we must simply combine both. In the first instance we need to define and clarify our realistic mental aptitude, define the real goal or goals, and then apply a positive aptitude in accordance with our true aptitude.

In this case, we are clear about what was our true aptitude, which goals we could achieve, and therefore our positive mental aptitude will be that our goals are achievable because they are realistic, and not impossible like they were at the beginning.

If we use this technique to ensure a realistic mental aptitude, we will achieve a well-being appropriate to our situation, and consequently we'll be in a happier mood and all because we have got to know the realistic mental aptitude we must adopt.

A couple of years ago I met a young manat a café, thirty two or so, who was complaining about the fact that he'd been looking for a job for the last two or three years but could not find any. He didn't seem to be making much of an effort with his appearance: he was wearing a T-shirt that must have been black when new; a pair of dark jeans and a not particularly trendy pair of trainers, but what was most noticeable was his solemn and serious expression, with his gaze lost, and the head down. He was saying that he had a degree in computing and since he finished his studies he'd been trying to get a job in IT to no avail. He kept saying that he needed a job that he was tired of having no money to go on holidays, to buy designer clothes, a car and a long list of things that he could not achieve because of lack of money.

After talking to him for a long time, I asked him: Do you really want to work? With strong conviction he replied with a resounding: "Yes" I took my chance then to tell him about my theory.

I told him: "friend, you must change your mental aptitude; you need to acquire a realistic mental aptitude. Let me explain: the reality is that you don't find a job because you are looking exclusively for jobs directly related to your degree and studies, and evidently things are hard at this moment and there are very few opportunities open. Therefore you must change to a realistic mental aptitude if you want to find a job. You must search for any job that will allow you to

achieve your objectives, and those objectives must be realistic according to the situation you are in now. Your goal should be to find any job that will allow you to make some money that will help you continue looking for a job in IT. I mean, work at anything that comes your way but at the same time carry on looking for your ideal job. If you acquire a realistic mental aptitude and define realistic and achievable objectives, you will be successful, you will feel calmer, full of hope, positive and happy, and you'll be able to apply a more positive aptitude that you will share with those around you and you will create the necessary conditions to achieve your final goal, working on what you really like and what you studied for.

Ten months later I met the same young man at the same café and I told him I hadn't seen him in a long time, and he looked very different. He was wearing a red shirt with white designs in the collar and cuffs, really pretty, dressed in a pair of label jeans and trainers that were in the latest model and design, all well-known and expensive labels.

The young man's expression had also changed, and now he appeared calm and healthy, smiling slightly and with an air of confidence that had not been there the first time we met.

He looked me in the eyes, and with a sincere smile said: “Thank you for the conversation we had ten months ago or thereabouts.You can’t imagine how much you’ve helped me and supported me.You gave me a piece of advice that changed my life.”

The young man, very excited, began to tell me what had happened in the intervening months. He told me: “The day after we met, I started to look for jobs, in IT and in anything else, without much selecting. It wasn’t easy, but as I was not limiting my idea of a suitable job, the opportunities of finding something interesting multiplied by a thousand. Forty five days after we saw each other, a friend offered me a job as a waiter in a café he owned, and I happily accepted. The first real objective that I had set myself, finding a job, had been achieved. Whilst I was working at the bar, I carried on looking for IT jobs that was what I really liked, but still couldn’t find anything. With my first salary, I went to a shopping mall and bought myself some shirts, a pair of trousers and a pair of trainers, all known labels. My dress style changed and as a consequence my appearance improved. After three months of working, a client who was having breakfast, saw me with the top of the computer we used as a till open (the touch screen was not working and I was trying to repair it), and asked me if I knew IT. I evidently told him that yes, I had studied IT. The man, surprised to see me working there when I knew IT asked me: "Would you be interested in working in IT in my company? My company works in telemarketing and each operator has his/her own computer; that means we have seventy computers and the IT expert who worked with us has left for another company. Can I count on you?"

"Very surprised I said yes, and agreed to go by his company, which was in the same street as the café, the next afternoon. I talked to him in his office and fifteen days later I was working for his company. Only five months had passed since our conversation and I had achieved my objective of getting a job in IT, and with a very interesting salary. I don't have much more to tell. I've been working there for five months and I've just come back from buying my first car. So my friend, thank you very much for your words in our first conversation; they changed my life."

I was very happy for the young man, and for all that had happened to him. Evidently the change that had taken place was exceptional, but, why had all these changes taken place? Simply because he had changed to a realistic aptitude, setting himself realistic and achievable goals; he had changed his aptitude (his dress sense, improving his looks, and his facial expression, appearing happier); he had achieved a positive mental aptitude based in the changes produced as he achieved his realistic objectives.

In conclusion, if we want to change our situation, what we must do is stop, sit down, change to a realistic mental aptitude, and pick up a piece of paper and write down our more immediate and achievablerealistic objectives. Once we have those, it will be easier to obtain them and logically we'll change to a realistic positive mental aptitude that will allow us to achieve new objectives, improving our situation constantly, and this cycle can be repeated as many times as is convenient or necessary.

2. Realistic and achievable objectives.

We've discussed the importance of having a realistic positive mental aptitude; we've seen, through examples, the importance of having realistic and achievable objectives. Now we're going to see how we can set these realistic and achievable objectives.

It's no use to have a realistic positive mental aptitude if when we define our goals and objectives they are neither realistic nor achievable.

I was watching an excellent television documentary programme about an African tribe. In one of the scenes, the hunters go searching food for the village. Eight hunters set off with their spears and shields; the documentary narrated their hunt for a species of antelopes that grazed nearby. When they reached the plain where the animals were eating, they advanced silently. At that moment, they see how the animals set off running and they follow in pursuit. One of the hunters realises that an antelope has trippedon the branch of a tree and fallen down, and although it quickly stands up and carries on running it's evident that it's hurt one of its legs as it's holding it in a strange posture and seems to be only running with the other three legs. That makes him slower than the rest of the herd. The hunters realise and abandon the rest of the antelopes focusing on running after the injured one. As it cannot run as fast as he was running before the fall, the hunters quickly catch up with him, throw him some spears and manage to kill it.

What a simple example of applied realistic mental aptitude, don't you think? The realistic mental aptitude of the hunters was to obtain food for the tribe; the objective was to hunt antelopes, but once they arrived where the antelopes were, and seeing that one of them had been injured, they decided to run after it as it would be easier to catch it and kill it.

The hunters changed their objective as they hunted, deciding to go after the weakest animal that was not only a real objective, but also more achievable than the rest of the antelopes.

Let's imagine for a moment: a person wants to lose 10 kg (20 lbs. or so); he starts following a diet advised by a dietician. To being with he's enthusiastic, because he has a clear realistic

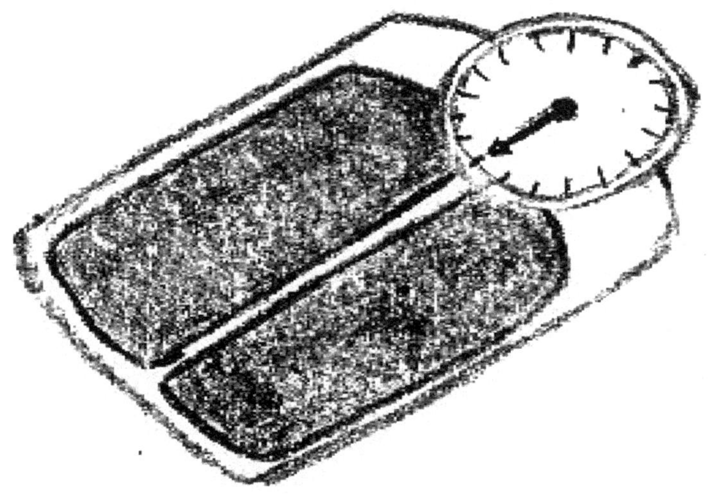

mental aptitude (he wants to lose weight to feel and look better), his objectives are clear; he wants to lose 10 kg. But what happens is the following: a week later, he's only lost 500g (a pound), and he wanted to lose weight quickly. Disappointed, he gets anxious, sad and loses heart and that affects him in the second week of dieting, to the point where he doesn't lose any weight at all. He has not followed the dietician's recommendations and he has even put back 100g of the weight he had lost the first week.

In this case, what happened is that the objective of losing 10kg was a realistic objective, it can be done, but it was not a realistic achievable objective, at least impossible to achieve in a week.

He needed to change his realistic objective to one that was also achievable: for instance, a better option would have been to set as an objective to lose 500g weight every week, to be consistent, follow the dietician's recommendations and decide that the realistic achievable objective would be to lose the 10kg in five months. If he had chosen this realistic achievable objective from the beginning he would not have been disheartened and he would have achieved his final objective after a few months.

This means that we have to be conscious of our limitation in each moment and we must adapt our realistic achievable objectives. We first must set up the easiest goals to achieve, and when we have achieved those we can aim for slightly more difficult goals, but they muststill remain achievable. We must remember that the sum of many small realistic achievable objectives will make us reach a bigger realistic achievable objective.

We must set our objectives clearly, and as we'll see in the next chapters we must then move into action and remain constant.

In a pre-match interview a sports journalist asked a football coach: "Do you think you'll win the championship?" His reply was quick, determined and realistic. He answered: "My objective is to win the next match, in a couple of weeks the next one, and so on and so forth. If we win all the matches then we'll be champions."

Evidently the coach had a realistic achievable objective, winning the match, and if he achieved all of his objectives, he would reach the final realistic and achievable objective, winning the championship.

The same happens to people who become successful in the world of business. If we think about big business men and women, we'll realise that to being with they all had a realistic positive aptitude. They started with small realistic achievable goals that slowly changed to more complex realistic achievable goals and eventually such strategy made them successful businessmen and women. I'm sure you can think of many successful businessmen and women who began with nothing and now have big fortunes.

We can also learn from successful people in other paths of life. Think for example of great singers. I'm sure you have a favourite singer who's very successful; do you think they became known and famous overnight? I'm sure you are aware that most singers build up their careers slowly, and obtain partial objectives before achieving a major success.

Another example would be elite sportsmen and women, for example athletes. Do you think they become champions straight away? Of course not. Training and working hard makes them progress and improve slowly, achieving small realistic objectives until they reach the final objective and success.

Hence it's very important to set realistic achievable objectives on the short-term, because if we manage to achieve them, we will feel encouraged, we'll have a realistic mental aptitude and it will give us a positive mental aptitude. We'll feel better, brighter, more ready to do things, and all this will allow us to achieve our final realistic goal. In summary, we'll achieve the success we've been looking for.

When we set our realistic achievable objectives we must analyse what type they are. We can easily divide them into two types, the partial realistic achievable objectives and the final one, in such a way that the sum of all the partial ones allows us to reach the final one.

There's a Spanish expression that translates: 'each and every single brick makes the wall'. A single brick is not a wall, but you need to put many together to make a wall.

We need to do the same. We have to set ourselves partial realistic achievable objectives, and when we reach them, the sum of all of them will take us to our final goal. When we use this technique and start achieving partial objectives, we feed our mind with positive energy, we are more optimistic about our chances, and realise that with each and every partial objective achieved we're a step closer to our final goal.

Many people join a gym to improve their looks and tone their bodies, but very few achieve their objectives. Do you know why? It's very simple. When we join a gym we have set ourselves a realistic achievable objective, obtaining a fitter and better body, but when we've been attending the gym for a few weeks, we realise that our progress is much slower than we had hoped for, and this creates a negative frame of mind.We get more and more disillusioned, and finally we stop going. Our final achievable objective has evaporated. If we plan instead partial realistic achievable objectives, as we go on achieving them we feel encouraged, we see how slowly and week by week our body tone improves, our muscle definition gets better, and with patience and commitment, adding up our partial realistic objectives we'll eventually reach our final goal, that is moulding our body as we like. This is the big difference between those who achieve their goals at the gym and those who don't. The first ones are constant, consistent and set themselves realistic achievable goals in the short-term and a final realistic achievable goal. The ones that never succeed only set themselves a final realistic achievable goal, and because the results aren't as fast as they'd expected they get disheartened and give up.

We can make a comparison between planning realistic achievable objectives and the Tour de France. The realistic achievable objectives in the Tour would be to obtain the best time each day, and the final realistic achievable objective is to have achieved the fastest time overall.

Therefore, after acquiring a realistic mental aptitude, we'll decide which realistic achievable objectives we should obtain in order to reach the final realistic achievable objectives.

3. Take Action.

We have learned the importance of having a realistic mental aptitude to be able to set ourselves partial and final realistic achievable objectives, but in this chapter, we will learn the importance of taking action to achieve those objectives.

According the Oxford Dictionary the definition of "action" is: the fact or process of doing something, typically to achieve an aim. Also, the thing done, an act.

If we have our realistic achievable objectives clearly defined, the next important step is to do something to achieve them; we must think and seek all those actions that will get us to achieve them.

In our lives, most of the things that happen to us are a result of things we have done. If we do nothing we will achieve nothing. I remember a friend once told me: "The person who does nothing, achieves nothing. The person who does something can achieve something." That is a self-evident truth, but although we all know the importance of "doing something" to reach our objectives, many times we just wait for them to happen, without moving a finger, as if expecting a miracle.

An example. I'm sure you've heard many times the typical: "how lucky that guy that won a million pounds in the lottery." Let's analyse this example. The person had an objective, he wanted to win money in the lottery, to reach that goal the most important thing he had to do was take action, he filled a ticket, paid for it, and made sure he submitted it in time. It's extremely rare to get any money the first time one plays the lottery, maybe this man had been playing for years, but he reached his objective because he took action, and probably because he was consistent and had been playing for a long time (in the next chapter we will see the importance of being consistent and committed). Of course it's impossible to win the lottery if you never play. If you don't undertake the action of playing you will never win.

Another example. A clothes shop was being sold because it had hardly any clients left. After a few days a young couple rented the shop. They set themselves a realistic achievable objective; in the first instance they wanted the shop to bring them enough money to improve their quality of life. Their next step was therefore to attract some clients. To achieve that they decided to stock articles of clothing with a unique and cheap price and reasonable quality. They thought about how to publicise the shop, and decided to distribute leaflets to all the houses in the neighbourhood, informing them of the advantages of their products (unique affordable price, quality, design and modernity). They had to do the distribution themselves, as they had no money left for staff after their investment. The next thing they did was tell all their friends so they could in turn tell their friends and people they knew that there was this shop with the characteristics already described. They used social media and the internet to do that (as it was the fastest and cheapest method). They continued with those strategies for a long time; they were constant and consistent in their actions and the shop became successful, its popularity grew, and two years later, they had five shops in the same city. They had been successful, and still better, they had achieved their objectives. Their quality of life was much better than before they embarked on the shop, and they had not only managed to make a living out of the business, but had been successful beyond their wildest expectations.

What happened that made this young couple so successful?

First, they had a realistic mental aptitude. They knew that a conventional clothes shop, with expensive prices would not work in the current social and financial situation (economic crisis), and that made them change the type of articles sold and the philosophy of the business, focusing on attracting as large a number of clients as possible. They also defined realistic objectives: being able to make a living of the business, to get enough money. With all that, the only thing left was taking action, seeking strategies that would allow them to make themselves known within their means, without having to spend lots of money, and applying those strategies with consistency and true commitment, applying a realistic mental attitude and this combination resulted in a great success.

Do you think they were lucky? What would have happened if they had not taken action? Probably they wouldn't have been successful if on

opening their business they hadn't done anything; if they had opened the business and had not advertised themselves their probabilities of achieving their goal would have been extremely limited, therefore they did something very important, they defined their objectives and they took action.

We must be very aware of the importance of having a realistic mental aptitude, of setting realistic and achievable objectives, and of taking action.

Once we reach this point, many of you will be wondering: And how can I know which actions to take to be able to achieve my objectives? I'll offer some advice.

When we're children, we get used to learning from those older than us, from our grandparents, our parents, our relatives in general, at school from our teachers, and we realised we're always learning from those around us, so why shouldn't we learn from those people who have reached success or from the businesses and companies that are successful?

In the example of the clothes shop, it's very likely that the young couple took notice of those clothes shops that were successful; they would have seen that these shops invested in publicity to become well known and triumph, but more important is that once they became aware of what other successful businesses were doing, they applied it to their cases but making adjustments to their circumstances. Evidently they didn't have the means to organise huge and expensive publicity campaigns, but they could adjust the idea to their resources and try and find effective and affordable versions. They knew from the very beginning due to their realistic objectives that their actions also had to be in keeping with reality and their means. And of course they were constant, they applied a realistic mental aptitude because their plan was perfectly designed and they believed in themselves.

We can also define the actions we need to

do by analysing the methods we have available. For example, if a chef has to prepare a meal for ten people, he will have to be ready with all the ingredients needed to prepare the dishes in their right amount. He'll make sure he does not miss any and he will cook with all the ingredients required to achieve the expected dish. But if he realises in time that he is missing some ingredients, he will likely change the menu and cook instead a dish with the ingredients he has, and because of his professionalism and his imagination he will still achieve a satisfying dish for all his guests.

In summary, if we have clearly defined realistic objectives, we also need to take realistic actions according to our means, and apply necessary modifications or corrections to achieve our goal.

I advise you to always have paper and pen handy (or use your phone or tablet), to write down all the actions that will allow you to achieve your objectives, and once you've written them down you must analyse which ones you can achieve within your means, and from that moment on you will be ready to take action.

Many readers will ask themselves: what do I do if I don't have any means with which to take action? If that is the case the answer is very simple. The realistic mental aptitude might have worked, you might have used it correctly, but where you have failed is in defining real objectives. In that case, like the chef, you need to rectify, you must set other partial and final realistic objectives, in accordance with the means you have. Then you'll realise your mistake.But when you apply new actions, you will see how the system works, and this is simply because you have applied correctly all the steps described so far.

Let's remind ourselves of the case of the IT expert we met in the first chapter. The objective mental aptitude was correct, he wanted to work but he realised it would be difficult to get a job working in IT.He defined partial and achievable realistic objectives, he sought any kind of job in order to achieve them, took action, used several tools, the first one was to talk to people to try and find a job, and this made one of his friends come forward with a job. He continued sending CVs applying for IT jobs, but as he was not successful, he went back to the first action that had worked for him, the spoken word. He talked to a client of the café who asked him if he knew IT and he answered "yes" and that gave him the chance he'd been looking for, he achieved his final achievable realistic objective. The method worked, but it worked because he followed all the steps without making any mistakes, he used the tools he had in his toolbox (the spoken word and the CVs), and he used both of them simultaneously.

Some time ago and acquaintance told me a story about a farmer. Here it is: “13 miles from a nearby village there was a farmer planting some vegetables in one of his fields. A young man came from behind him, stopped there and asked him how long it would take him to reach the village. The farmer turned around, looked at him and told him he didn’t know how long it would take him. The young man shrugged and started walking again. When he’d walked a few steps, the farmer told him, shouting, “it will take you two hours”, the young man turned and thanked him.”

What happened? Why didn’t he reply when he was first asked? It’s very simple. The farmer didn’t see the young man arrive. He had to wait until he started walking again to realise at what pace he walked and then he was able to work out how long it would take him to get to the village.

Until the young man took the action of walking, the farmer didn't know how long it might take him to get to his destination, as he didn't know how he walked.

What I'm trying to say is that until you take action, until you start the journey you don't know how difficult it will be to reach your destination. You need to apply these steps with confidence, analyse the situation, acquire a realistic mental aptitude, define achievable realistic objectives and with the tools you have available you must take action. The next step in order to achieve our realistic achievable objectives is to be constant.

4. Be Constant

When I was a child my grandmother told me a story that taught me a great deal and I'd like to share it with you.

"Many years ago, there was a river with water so transparent and clean that two villages used to go to collect water to drink for themselves and their animals. The river was in the valley between two big mountains, and on top of each mountain sat one of the villages. Every day they had to go down to the river to collect the water.

The first village was called Constantville and the other one, at the other side of the river Inconstantville.

After a hot summer, the two mayors of the villages met to discuss how they could transport the water to each one of the villages without having to have to constantly go up and down the mountains. After hours and hours of meetings, and debating different options, the two mayors decided to create a net of pipes and ducts reaching each one of the villages with a manual water pump in the central square of the village to pump the river water up, and save themselves the 2 miles distance between the villages and the river.

They started work straight away: in Constantville they began to assemble the pipes towards their village, and the same did the inhabitants of Inconstantville.

They worked very hard throughout the months of autumn and winter, with the intention of finishing the installation before the arrival of the summer high temperatures.

Both villages achieved one of their objectives. By mid Spring the pipes had reached the centre of the village. They designed a beautiful fountain, and in order to bring the water from the river they installed a water pump. At the time water pumps were approximately one metre tall, with a strong handle that one had to push and pull up and down, therefore suctioning the water and bringing it up the pipes to the village.

The inhabitants of Constantville and Inconstantville were very happy, and they threw a huge party that started in the evening and did not finish until the early hours of the morning.

Next day, when all the inhabitants of both villages were awake and in the square by the fountain, they began to pump the handle of the water pump, to try and bring the water up from the river. They decided to take turns: each neighbour would be pumping for ten minutes in the village fountain.

Both villages were full of enthusiasm and they started very strong. All the inhabitants took turns first, then took a second round, and another, and another, and carried on until the early hours of the morning. But the people of Inconstantville decided to stop at 2 a.m. and go back the next day. By contrast in Constantville they carried on pumping until 5 a.m. and at that point water started flowing.

Constantville organised a party with dances, food, drink, and they made such a racket that their neighbours from Inconstantville woke up and could see the party taking place in the other village. They quickly realised that in Constantville they had managed to pump the water to the village.

The inhabitants of Inconstantville felt encouraged by the example of their neighbours and next morning started pumping. The problem was that as they'd stopped pumping the previous night before the water reached the fountain, the water had dropped back down to the river and they had to start again from the very beginning. They were pumping all day, but around midnight, tired of their efforts, they stopped and left it for the next day.

When they got up at 6 am they realised that again all their efforts had been in vain and the water had gone all the way back down to the river. They kept doing the same thing for several weeks, until one of the neighbours convinced the rest that they should not stop until the water reached the fountain.

This time they persevered and didn't stop until the water reached the fountain. The only drawback was that in the process they'd lost several days, although they also had a big party to celebrate that was enjoyed by the whole population.

In the meantime in Constantville, as they had access to water sooner, they could water their animals and their crops, and the citizens didn't waste their time going to the river to get water. As a result Constantville became a rich village in both agriculture and animal farming.

On the other hand Inconstantville had yet to develop their farming and agriculture and were lagging behind. And this is the story of the two villages, Constantville and Inconstantville."

A fabulous story that taught me the main principles of the realistic mental aptitude, of the realistic objectives and of the importance of being constant.

Let's analyse the previous story. Both villages had a realistic mental aptitude, they knew that going to get water to the river every day, was not only an effort, but it was not effective as they were limited in the amounts of water they were able to carry, and they planned as their realistic reachable goal, to join pipes from the river, up the mountain and to place a water pump and a fountain in the main square of the village. Perfect. It was a realistic achievable objective as they knew other villages used the same method to obtain water from nearby rivers. They quickly took action (remember the importance of doing something discussed in the previous chapter, and how you need take action to achieve your objectives).

Up to that point they were following the plan and going step by step in their way to achieving their objective. Then, what was the difference between Constantville and Inconstantville that made Constantville successful and left the other village with no water despite trying many times? It's very simple. What makes the difference between two people who use the same tools and have the same objective is simply being constant until you achieve your objective.

The inhabitants of the first village were constant and didn't stop pumping water until they obtained their objective, whilst in the second village every time they got tired, they abandoned and that made them have to start from the very beginning every day, wasting a precious time.

That was the big difference between the two villages and for that reason and that reason only the first village became prosperous much faster than the second.

However, we must not forget an important detail: the second village eventually also achieved its objective, and that teaches us two important things. First, that they rectified their behaviour, thanks to a neighbour, and decided not to stop pumping until the water reached the pump. The second point to learn is that if we have realistic achievable goals and we are constant we will eventually obtain them.

In the next chapter we'll see the importance of rectifying when it is required.

In summary, if we want to be successful in any mission, we must persevere, act with determination, work hard, be firm and in some cases even obsessive, be a bit stubborn and insistent, in two words, be constant.

I don't want to forget to comment on another lesson I learned from that story. Do you remember that the first village managed to get the water to the fountain at 5 am, whilst the second village stopped at 2 am? What does that tell us? That sometimes we don't achieve our objective because we're not constant enough when it's just within our reach. In this case it was only 3 hours pumping that made the difference.

You must be very mindful of this lesson. When we have decided on an objective, we must be constant enough to go all the way and achieve it. It's useless to begin the process of realistic mental aptitude, setting achievable realistic objectives and taking action, if we aren't going to be constant. We will have wasted our time and energy, and worse still, we won't have achieved our objective. That will make us frustrated and will lower our mood. We will be in a worse place than when we decided to change our life, a change for the better, to improve our circumstances. Although we started the process in the right mind-set by not being constant we ended up worse than when we started.

Being constant has been the key for the great majority of people who have achieved success, from sports personalities, to businessmen, entrepreneurs, researchers, and it is the key even in many everyday tasks and pursuits, like getting your dream romantic partner, finding a job, losing weight, completing your studies, and we could go on and on.

We have all heard how Thomas Alba Edison, in 1879, perfected the "incandescent light bulb". His initial objective was to obtain a filament that would reach incandescence without melting. After many attempts and the same number of failures, and with a filament that instead of being made of metal was made of carbonated bamboo, he managed to get his light bulb working and producing light for eight hours. We can see that he applied the technique we're studying. He had a realistic mental aptitude. He knew he would be able to obtain a light bulb with filament that didn't melt because he had all the necessary elements to try (the required tools that we talked about in the previous chapter). He set himself a realistic objective, he took action, he was constant, and as we've said before even stubborn. He rectified as many times as it was necessary after each failure, and eventually he was successful. It was his perseverance that made him achieve his goal.

It is fundamental to follow all the steps in the technique. You cannot jump or ignore any if you want to reach your final goal. It is of no use to acquire a realistic mental aptitude if we will not persevere and remain constant, because we might fail when we were just a step away from success. We had it within our reach but we were not constant enough and were left on the verge of success.

It will be a surprise for many to hear me say that we are born with the quality of being constant and that in many cases we lose it as we grow older, we become more conformist and get used to an easy life. Let me give you an example; often we see a child who wants something and he will insist time and again, sometimes even crying, and becoming difficult and tiring, many times succeeding in getting us to the point when we cannot bear any more crying and tantrums. What do we do in a case like that? Because of the pressure, nerves it all conspires to make us say yes in many occasions. The child has been constant; he knows his objective and uses the tools within his reach (crying, tantrums, etc.), and he uses them as many times and for as long as required to obtain his goal.

Let's take a bit of time and reflect about our own lives. Try to remember something you have achieved without the need of persevering, for example, you might remember when you saw that girl/or boy you liked and you wanted her (him) to be your girlfriend/boyfriend, I'm sure you had to remain constant to achieve your objective, or remember when you obtained your driving licence, I'm sure you had to study consistently to obtain it, or remember when you went on a trip with the savings of the whole year. You were constant and you saved over a long period to achieve your objective. And I'm sure there are many more examples you can come up with.

Before we move on to the next chapter, let's do a little exercise. We take a sheet of paper and divide it in three vertical columns. On the left we write down all the things we remember that we have achieved without having to remain constant. In the middle column we create a list with all the things we have achieved because of persevering. Finally, in the column on the right we jot down all the things we have not achieved because we have not been constant enough.

If the column on the right is longer than the other two, you are an inconstant person, and therefore you must change your aptitude to achieve your new goals. If on the other hand, the column in the middle is the longest one you are a constant person and you must remain the same. Finally, if the column on the left is the longest, you are a very lucky person, although I can tell you that till now I've never met a person whose left column is longer than the other two.

I also recommend you that you reflect if you have data in the list in the middle (the list of being constant), and in the list on the left (inconstant). This would indicate that in certain moments you have been constant but on other occasions you haven't, and you need to give it some thought. Why have you remained constant sometimes and inconstant other times? Probably because of hurdles and difficulties that made you lose motivation, or because you got tired of trying, you did not apply the corrections (we will analyse those in the next chapter), or maybe you didn't want to pay the price to achieve the objective. Sometimes we have to pay a price to achieve our objective, and the price might be material (money, things, etc.) or immaterial (effort, choice, suffering, tenacity, etc.). The price to pay to achieve our objective will also be the subject of a future chapter.

As we have seen, being constant is one of the keys to success. But remember it's not the most important. We must follow the technique, from beginning to end, from acquiring a realistic mental aptitude, up to being constant, without jumping any steps, as we have already explained in previous chapters.

5. Rectifications and adjustments.

We must learn the importance of rectifications, or we may also call them adjustments.

As we have already seen in previous chapters, once we have defined the realistic objectives and after taking action, if we see that instead of achieving our objectives we are deviating from them we must make the necessary adjustments.

Let's have a look at a very simple example to illustrate the point. A few days ago I was watching a car race. When it started it was cloudy, but the asphalt was completely dry. 30 minutes into the race it started to rain heavily. At that moment all the cars, one after another, began to enter boxes to change from the tyres for dry conditions (the ones they had on) to tyres for rain. The race carried on and there was stiff competition between first and second place. When there were ten laps left till the end it was clear that the first car had a better grip on the bends than the second one; that allowed it to slowly gain advantage. At that moment, the car in the second place decided to go to boxes and the mechanics adjusted the front wing, and it returned quickly to the race. I was surprised to see how very quickly it started shortening the distance with the first classified. It had gained better grip on the bends and that allowed him to get in and out of them faster. In the last lap, and to be more precise, in the last bend, he managed to overtake the car in first position and won the race.

We should analyse the example in more detail. The pilots in both cars had the same realistic mental aptitude: they were good pilots with excellent cars and they had set themselves a realistic achievable objective, to win the race. When it started to rain, they both realised that with a tyre for dry weather they would not be able to win the race because the car would lose adherence and they might even have an accident. They decided to rectify and they changed their tyres for others suited to wet weather conditions. But observe an important detail. The vehicle in the second place noticed that the one in first position was gaining distance mostly because it had better stability and grip on the bends, and that allowed it to enter the bends faster and with more stability, and at the same time, exit them faster. What did he do when he realised that? Very easy, he readjusted again, they modified the position of the front wing to gain in adherence and stability, and he was correct, he managed not only to reach the car in the first position but he overtook it and won the race.

It is an extremely clear example of the need to make the necessary rectifications and adjustments to reach our objectives.

When we have defined clearly our realistic and achievable objectives, if we see that we are deviating ourselves from the goals or simply we realise that we're not achieving them as quickly as we'd like, we must make the necessary adjustments or rectifications. We must not be afraid of rectifying, because these modifications are the ones that will allow us to reach our objectives.

Let's remember the example of the incandescent light-bulb. Thomas Alba Edison rectified as many times as was necessary in order to achieve his objective. He tried different types of materials to create the light-bulb filament, until he found one that would not melt. He wasn't afraid of making all the required modifications. He was constant, worked hard and persevered, but he also made all the changes necessary.

There is a saying in Spanish that would translate "rectifying wise men's virtue". It's true; we must all adjust our strategies until we achieve our goals. If we observe that we're not achieving the desired result, we must pause for a moment and make changes or adjustments, and that will allow us to achieve them more easily.

You must have realised that in our lives we must make adjustments very often, even in the most everyday activities. We can look at an example:

"When we're travelling in our car and we see that there is a traffic-jam in our planned route, on many occasions we'll change the route we take, trying a different road, that we might not have considered in the first instance because it is longer, but in this case it would be the preferable option to avoid the traffic-jam. We rectified our route to succeed in our goal that is to reach our destination as quickly as possible.”

“The chefs and cooks, those professionals of the culinary arts that create for us those wonderful dishes, very often whilst cooking will try the food and notice that it needs a bit more salt and they will add a teaspoon on. They are applying the same principle we’ve been discussing. If it doesn’t have enough salt, they add a bit more until it had the perfect taste.”

“Children are also great experts in rectifying. As we have observed before, when

children want something, whatever it might be, they will use all the techniques they know to try and achieve their objective. When a child wants something, he might first ask for it. If his mother and father don't give it to him, he will change his tactic and will start crying. If that is not sufficient he will modify it further and carry on crying but also start kicking. If that doesn't work either, he will cry, kick out, throw himself on the floor, become a pest, etc. On occasions they will change their aptitude and will start giving us kisses, hugs, caresses, and they will carry on modifying their technique until they achieve their objective. I'm sure you're familiar with this scenario, be it because you're a mother or father, or because of nieces, nephews, or the children of friends who use such technics. Or you might simply still remember what you did when you were children."

Therefore, we must not be scared of rectifying. We must remember that the most important thing is to reach our realistic objective, and it doesn't matter how many times we must rectify. The most important thing is to realise that on many occasions we'll have to make changes, and not because we've made a mistake in our strategy, or with the tools we're using, and we must never think that something has failed. If we have followed all the steps of "the realistic mental aptitude" nothing can go wrong. We have defined achievable objectives; we're using the appropriate tools we have at our disposal. In that case if we must make rectifications it's only because sometimes circumstances change, sometimes something unpredictable happens or the circumstances have changed at the same time as we were taking action to achieve our objectives. Whatever the reason, we must be aware that rectifying is only one step we must adopt to reach our objectives, to be successful.

I can assure you that rectifying is never a step back, but a step forward, and therefore if every time we make an adjustment we're moving forward, we'll be closer and closer to reaching our real objective.

I remember a friend who has a bar in a neighbouring town. When he opened the bar, he decided it would be solely a tapas bar. Initially it was going very well, but because of specific circumstances, the business started to lose clients, and it worsened every day. From the very opening of the bar he'd never wanted to offer sandwiches or a fixed menu, and he always closed a day per week. Evidently his objective was to have a functioning and successful business, but something was not working. He stopped to think and decided to try something different. He incorporated sandwiches, fixed menus and his famous tapas. He also decided to make sacrifices and opened every day. From that moment on he observed that his clientele was more varied, and that kept him busier with more income, achieving his objective that was simply to have a well-functioning business.

From the moment my friend decided to modify his strategy, his business has been functioning as he wanted it to. He was not afraid to make changes, because he knew what his objective was, and he was prepared to pay the price to achieve it, the price being sacrificing his day off, and that gave him another day of weekly income. In sum, he did not only rectify, but also paid the price required to be successful.

6. Paying the Price

We are used to paying a price for all the things we want. When we go to a department store or a supermarket to buy food, clothes, books, or any number of things, we always have to pay the required price.

If we want to open a business we'll have to pay the rent; we'll need to get the required permits and pay taxes; we'll need to get necessary furniture; obtain the products we want to sell and so on.

As we see we're prepared to pay the price for the things we want

We're all familiar with the saying: "What wouldn't I give to have this or that?"

With that in mind, I'm going to ask you a question: how much would you be prepared to pay to achieve all the objectives you have set for yourself? I'm also going to ask you: What would you be prepared to pay to be successful? And the last question I have for you: Has anybody ever told you that life is easy, that success is a child's play, and that you don't have to do anything in order to achieve your objectives? The answer is no. Nobody has ever told you such a thing.

The price we have to pay to achieve our goals and become successful can be material or immaterial. By material price I mean that it can be obtained using something tangible, for example money, products, articles, and similar things. By immaterial I refer to intangible things, for example, effort, sacrifice, being constant (that as you'll remember we have discussed at length in a previous chapter), patience, tenacity, suffering, and a very long list.

If we focus on having to pay the price to achieve our goals by material means, we can easily bring to mind examples of things that have happened around us all of our lives. A friend called Eduardo, who was a driving instructor and had been working in the same business for twenty years, had always dreamed of having his own driving school. It was his aspiration and utmost desire. His objective was to be self-employed, and he knew he had the necessary knowledge and experience to make it a success. He looked for an appropriate site to rent for the business; he talked to car dealers. Once he got an address for the business he got an expert to prepare a business plan. When he got the report from the experts that showed a positive outlook for his business, he sold an apartment he owned, and he used the money as investment for his new business. He worked very hard. To begin with, as he could not afford to hire any extra staff, he did all the work himself. He was working 15 hours per day, but the effort was worth it because finally he achieved his goal. Now he has six people working for him at the driving school, the business is doing well and he's very proud of his success.

My friend Eduardo paid the price to achieve his objective. First he had to pay the material price. With the money from selling his property he got the investment necessary to start up the business. But more than that, as you'll have noticed, he had to pay also a very important immaterial price. How? With his effort, being constant, sacrificing himself, working hard many hours a day, spending lots of time in the business instead of having more time with his family, but finally, after paying the price, the most important thing is that he achieved his goal, he was successful in his business. He made his dream come true.

In a previous chapter we saw the importance of being constant, but we should not forget the importance of paying the price required to achieve our objectives, to make our dreams become realities.

On many occasions we realise that the main difference between a successful person and one who does not succeed, is simply that the first one was prepared to pay any price necessary to achieve success, whilst the second wasn't.

When I finished High School, some of my female friends decided to study to become nurses and complete their nursing degrees. The objective of my friends was to work in a hospital as nurses. That was their dream and vocation. They studied hard, completed the degree and obtain their desired qualification. When they finished their studies they took action to achieve their final goal.

They started looking for jobs in the town where they lived, but they soon realised that there were

no jobs for them there, it was nearly impossible to obtain the position they desired. They did not get disheartened though. Their goal and dream remained alive in their minds. They modified their plan and started to look for jobs farther away, in other town and cities (changing to a mental realistic aptitude). They were so constant and enthusiastic that soon they had a job offer. They had a chance to work in a hospital, nearly 300 miles away from their homes. They did not hesitate. They decided to move and start working in a hospital in the new city. They had to leave behind their families (parents and siblings), and for one of them it was particularly hard, as she had a steady boyfriend.They had bought a house, were planning to get married, and having to leave all that behind was very hard. But they were so keen on achieving their dream that they were prepared to pay the price required. They moved to the new city and started working there. They are still working there to this day. The one who had a boyfriend paid a particularly high price. The relationship cooled down and ended, but luckily she met somebody else, a person prepared to share her dream. Today, they're happily married, have gorgeous children, their husbands support them, and most importantly, their dream became true and they can share it with their families.

There were other peers who also studied nursing like my friends, but decided to stay in our city. They tried to find work but did not find many opportunities. They were aware that if they moved to a different location they would likely find a job, but they were not prepared to pay such a price. They did not want to leave their families behind to achieve their dream, and in the end they did not get to work as nurses.

This is a clear example of why some people achieve their dream and are successful, and others don't. Some are prepared to pay the price, but others are not.

In that last example we can see that the price they had to pay was not material. On the contrary, it was intangible. They paid the price with enthusiasm, firm determination, with pain and suffering, as they had to abandon their families, and of course with the conviction that they were doing what they had to in order to achieve their dream.

The majority of elite sportsmen and women were born of humble families, but that was no obstacle for them to achieve their objectives and become successful. Why? Because they paid the price. Most of them sacrificed their childhood, training hard, whilst children their age were playing games or going to parties. Instead of enjoying themselves they were always training, sacrificing many of the things people normally do at their ages. They paid the price required to achieve their dream, in their case success in their chosen sport. I'm sure you can think of the name of quite a few well known sports' personalities, both national and international, that fit the bill.

Let's take a moment to summarise the information we have shared from chapter one up to now. As you now know, the technique of the mental realistic aptitude consists of a series of actions or steps to follow. In the first chapter we saw what a mental positive aptitude is and its importance. Then we learned how to define partial achievable realistic objectives and final achievable realistic objectives. Once we have defined our objectives we saw how important it is to take action. Then we reflected on the importance of being constant and not abandoning before achieving success. We also discussed the importance of taking stock and making the necessary rectifications and modifications if circumstances change. In this chapter we talked about paying the price required to achieve our dreams and also the different types of prices, material and immaterial.

Do you want to know which one of these steps is the most important?

All of them are important, because you must follow all the steps in the technique of mental realistic aptitude if you want to be successful. But I must tell you that it's very important that you understand this chapter, 'paying the price', well and accept its content, for a very simple reason. If you follow all the steps we have discussed but you are not prepared to pay the price you will never achieve your objectives, you won't be successful. Because of that we will discuss it in more detail, not because this chapter is the most important, but because it is one of the final required steps to achieve any goals you have set.

We are talking about what 'paying the price' to achieve success means. We have looked at examples and observed that the payment might be by material or immaterial means. I organised a seminar where one of the participants was telling another one: "what they're telling us here is all very well and good; the theory appears logical and easy, but it doesn't work for me. I want to open a second-hand car dealership, but I have no money to rent the premises, or to buy second-hand cars to sell them later to my costumers, and therefore I think this theory is of no use to me. How am I going to pay the price when I have no money?" I approached him and told him: "my friend, I don't think you've understood the technique I have explained in the seminar. In first place I explained what the mental realistic aptitude is. After listening to your comments I believe you're mistaken. Your real situation is that you want to have a business buying and selling cars, but you don't have cars. I will suggest to you a plan that applies the principles of the realistic mental aptitude. You should consider starting the business without vehicles or premises. You could start by simply contacting people who would be prepared to sell you their car. At the same time you offer it to people who might be interested in buying it. Your partial achievable objective should be selling a few cars. With the money you obtain that way, you can buy a low price vehicle as an investment, and take your time to sell it at the best possible price. You keep on doing this until you have accumulated a number of cars.

Take action. As you don't have much money to launch your business, you can advertise your cars through the internet (social networking sites, free advertisements or listings, etc.). You must dedicate as much time as necessary to the task, and if you are constant you'll see that you've created a snowball effect that will be unstoppable. If you notice something is not working well, you can make the necessary modifications. For example, if free advertisements on the internet don't suffice, you can always produce and distribute leaflets advertising your enterprise. You can leave them on parked cars saying you buy and sell second-hand vehicles. And finally, you must pay the price to achieve your objectives, to have your own business. You'll have to work hard, sacrificing your free time for the business, and if you apply all of these steps, I'm sure you'll achieve what you wish. You must realise something very important. The final goal you had described and the goal achieved by applying my plan are one and the same. The only difference is that you had not applied a realistic mental aptitude. If you don't have enough capital to invest you cannot have as a realistic goal to open you own business in your own premises. You must start slowly, with partial objectives and finally you'll achieve your goal.

It's no excuse to say that because we don't have money we can't do anything. The problem is that our goals are not realistic.

I was very lucky to meet Doña AmaliaMinaya and I'm going to tell you her story:

"She was born in 1920, in a village in the province of Cuenca (Spain).She got married in 1938, with the Civil War in full swing, with an officer of one of the two sides of the war (I don't specify with army he was fighting for, as it's not relevant to the rest of the story).Her husband used to come and go due to the fighting and spent long periods of time away from her. She got pregnant when she was still only 18 and the 2nd of January 1939 her daughter was born. The Spanish Civil War officially ended on the 1st April 1939. Her husband, who had been fighting in the front line never came back (he was declared missing in action). He never got to meet his daughter. At the time everybody knew everybody in the village.

When the winning army entered the village, very quickly those who supported them gave them information about the people who had been affiliated to the other side. Evidently, the troops were soon told that she was the wife of one of the officers of the other side.

Before the troops of the winning army came looking for her to arrest her, and with the help of some relatives and the nuns from a nearby convent, she left for Valencia with her little daughter in her arms. Her baby was only a few months old and she hardly had any money. When she arrived in Valencia, she went to visit some people she knew from her village who had moved there, hoping they could keep the girl with them whilst she went looking for a job. Her money was running out and that meant she had to find a job and fast. A few days later, with no money left to speak of, sleeping on the floor at her friends' house, looking after her baby daughter but with hardly anything to feed her with (it was the postwar period and everything was scarce unless you had money to pay the huge prices of the black market), she found a job cleaning rooms for prostitutes in the red-light district in Valencia.

Slowly she managed to get other cleaning jobs, improving her position, and ending up working for some of the most important people in Valencia's society.

She learned to read and write, by reading the advertisements on the walls and the names in the shop-windows. She learned to add-up and subtract slowly, with the help of friends and neighbours.

She made sure her daughter had a good education, giving her not only the basic studies but ensuring she was formally educated like a young girl of a good family. She made sure that her daughter never lacked anything, although they were never well-off, up to the moment when her daughter got married.

She worked all her life, improving continuously until, when she was already seventy, she had to retire due to ill health and got the corresponding pension. By then she had remarried, and her second husband, Andrés, was a wonderful man and they had been together for over twenty years. She became a widow aged seventy seven.

She always overcame all the obstacles in her life, always fighting with energy, with character and illusion. She lived through very hard times, but she also had very happy moments.

She enjoyed the company of her daughter, husband and grandchildren. And when she was 90 years old, only two months to become 91, on the 25th December 2010 (Christmas Day) she passed away. She died convinced that she had achieved all her objectives that were to be happy and to make her family happy: her husband, daughter and grandchildren."

This is the story of that wonderful woman called AmaliaMinaya, the happiest person I've ever met, the most dedicated to others, the most generous, the hardest fighter. She was my grandmother, the person who taught me, for the first time, the technique of the mental realistic aptitude. She did it without knowing it, with her actions, and by her example, as I saw how she behaved throughout her life.

Let's check how my grandmother Amalia applied the mental realistic aptitude. In first place, she was fully aware of her circumstances. She knew she had left her village to go to Valencia that she was alone with her daughter and she hardly had any money. Her first partial realistic objective was to find any job that would allow her to feed her daughter. Her final achievable realistic objective, she planned to slowly progress and get better jobs until she could reach a situation that would allow her to live with dignity and to create a good family life. As soon as she arrived in Valencia she took action, she started looking for any available jobs. She found first one, and progressively and step by step, being constant, she changed jobs, improving her job situation. She rectified and made modifications as many times as was necessary, constantly improving her status, and of course, she had to pay the price to achieve her objectives. And as I've already said, she reached her final realistic achievable objective: to be happy and to make her family happy all her life, up to the point of her death.

You have read examples of people who have paid the price necessary to achieve their objectives. We have analysed some where the price to pay had been material and some others where it had been immaterial. In reality, in most cases the price to pay will be immaterial (effort, suffering, tenacity, sacrifice, etc.), in a percentage of cases the price will be both immaterial and material (we've also seen some examples), and in very few cases only material.

II PART

ANEX

7. Knowing what you don´t want.

Are you surprised by the title of this chapter? I'm sure that if you've reached this point in your reading is because you are very clear about what you want. I'm sure you want to change things in your life, you aspire to improve things, you want to reach success, you want to be the best at all you do, and many more things.

However, as my great friend Vicente González used to say, in each and every moment of our lives it becomes more difficult, and therefore more important, to know what we don't want, in order to be sure of what we want.

To have a mental realistic aptitude it's very important to know what we don't want for our lives. The key and main reason for this is simple. If I ask you what you want, you will quickly give me a long list with all the things you wish for and desire. But if instead I ask you to make a list with all the things you don't want for yourself, would you be able to?

Let's do an exercise. In a piece of paper you are going to create a list with all the things you want in life. In this list you will name, in order of importance for you, everything you want in relation to: love, work, friendship, family and studies, to name but a few. You'll see how easy it is to start scribbling everything you want under each one of the suggested headings. They will quickly come to your mind and you'll put them down in paper, with hardly any doubts.

Now, in the same piece of paper, but on the other side, you're going to write another list with the same headings, and also in order of importance, but now you need to write down everything you don't want for this aspects of your life.

If you have followed my instructions and completed the simple exercise, I'm sure that in contrast with the first list, where you started writing straight away and without hesitation, for the second list you will have needed more time to think before starting writing. Not only that, but once you are writing it down, doubts will come to your mind and you'll wonder if these are really the things you don't want and you won't be sure either of the order you are using to prioritise them.

Also, you will see that the first list is longer than the second. Do you know why? The answer is pure logic. From the moment we're born we get used to being asked what we want. For example, between the ages of 10 and 14 how many times did they ask you: What do you want to do when you're a grown up? I'm sure they never asked you what you didn't want to be when you grew up. I'm certain that people have asked you more than once if you want to be rich, or successful, or happy.

These two lists you have composed you must keep safe, because you will need them to set off on the road to success.

When you have clearly defined what you don't want in your life, you'll have reached the point when you must apply a realistic mental aptitude for each one of the concepts you have written down. When you're sure of what you don't want, it is much easier to define the priorities for the things you really want, and it will become easier to set achievable realistic objectives.

Recently I did an impromptu study. I decided to go out on the streets and I asked two questions to randomly chosen people:

1st Question: What do you want for your life? People always replied very quickly to this question, and answered by telling me: money, love, health, to be rich, to be happy, a sports car or a high standing position in the workplace, etc.

2nd Question: What don't you want for your life? To answer this, people always had to stop and think. Strangely enough a large majority of people would reply by telling me: "I don't know" and after thinking about it a bit longer, they would reply with: Well, I don't want to be ill, or I don't want anything bad to happen to my family, or I don't want to lose my job, etc.

By completing this small study I reached two conclusions: first, that we don't know with certainty what we don't want and to begin with we're very doubtful of our answers, and second, that when we come to think about what we don't want, we are no longer materialistic, and we're more concerned about our wellbeing and that of those around us. In summary, we think about our heath and the health of our friends and family.

I was talking to a friend of mine, who had divorced her husband, some time ago, and I asked her: "Why did you get divorced?" She was very quick in replying that she got divorced because the relationship with her husband wasn't good, they hardly talked to each other, they were forever fighting, they didn't feel happy together, and the most important reason (and that was what really surprised me), she told me she had got divorced, because she didn't want to live the rest of her life in such a relationship and with that kind of life as a couple.

My friend's answer is rather curious. If you notice, in her reply to begin with what she does is justify the reasons for her divorce (she didn't feel happy, the relationship wasn't good, etc.) whilst at the end she gave me the real reason for the divorce. She had realised what she did not want for the rest of her life. Once this became clear, she applied a mental realistic aptitude; she set the achievable realistic objective of being happy, and took action: she divorced her husband.

In this example you can see the importance of knowing what one does not want. Once we are clear about what we don't want, we act quickly, with more determination, with more confidence, and this will allow us to acquire a realistic mental aptitude.

Let's look at another example. Another friend of mine, who runs a bar, had problems with alcohol around a year ago, he was also taking illicit substances on occasions, and both things were ruining both his health and the running of the business. Luckily, with the help of his family and some friends, he realised that he didn't want to spend the rest of his life like that, because in the end he would end up an alcoholic and would destroy his business. Once he realised what he did not want, he went to a specialised detoxification centre to treat his addictions, convinced that he could change, and with the help of professionals, he managed to leave all his addictions behind, and nowadays he is doing well, he's healthy and his business is going from strength to strength.

This is another clear example of how powerful and strong a motivation knowing what we don't want can be. In this case my friend did not want to be ill and dependent on his addictions, he realised that nothing good would come out of it. My friend changed to a mental realistic aptitude. His achievable realistic objective was to stop his addictions. He took action (he followed professional advice); he was constant in not giving up despite the difficulties and crisis; he

paid the price (he had to deal with anxiety, symptoms of withdrawal, feeling physically ill, cravings, etc.), but finally he achieved his objective and was successful .

This shows us that we need to realise the importance of knowing what we don't want, that can be even more important than knowing what we want.

8. Patience.

Patience is a human virtue. We need to know how to use it in order to achieve our objectives and be successful.

We have already looked at how important it is to be constant to be able to apply the technique of “the realistic mental aptitude”. As you must know, patience is closely linked to constancy. It is extremely difficult to be constant if we’re not patient. The reason is self-evident. When we follow the steps in this book, we must be clear that the results might not be as quick as we’d like, and that could make us impatient. In turn this could have a negative impact on our character, that will no longer be positive, we will be in a bad mood, we will become frustrated and the combination of all these factors can make us forget the importance of remaining constant and we might abandon our efforts before reaching our final achievable realistic objective.

We should never mistake patience with being passive. I'll explain myself. You will remember that one of the steps of the technique was to "rectify". If we are constant, we apply all the steps we have learned, and we realise we're not achieving our objectives, we should not become passive. It's going to be very difficult to achieve our goals if our aptitude is passive.

On many occasions, in everyday situations we have been impatient, and as a result we not only have not achieved our goals, but sometimes we have made matters worse for ourselves, even gone backwards, wasting time, opportunities and maybe even money.

Let's see an example of patience applied. "A little while ago I heard on the TV that there was going to be a concert by an internationally renowned singer, the only one in this country. As you can imagine there were long queues of fans at the door of the concert hall from a week before the event. The reason for the queues was that all those people wanted to be amongst the first ones to go into the concert hall and position themselves close to the stage, to be able to have a better view of their idol. And of course, those who had been queuing the longest went in first and managed to be close to their favourite singer."

In this example it's easy to see how the technique of the realistic mental aptitude has been applied. In the first place, the fans knew there would be lots of people. Those who were waiting had an achievable realistic objective that was to see their idol close-up. They took action and went to the concert hall a week before the event to queue at the door. They were constant and patient for seven days; they paid the price, both material and immaterial. The material price was evidently the price of the ticket, and the immaterial, much harder, was the sacrifice of spending seven days basically living in the streets, eating and drinking outdoors, being cold at night, and even having to put up with rain a few days, but finally they achieved their goal, they could watch their favourite singer from the first row and some fans even managed to hug him and kiss him. In sum they triumphed, they were successful.

By contrast now I'll show you an example of impatience. Last Christmas there was the launch of a new model of a very well-known games console. It was the perfect present for the occasion and a big department store located in the vicinity of my house had a fantastic offer on the games console. For five days they would be selling it with fifty per cent discount. It was a great offer and a huge saving. A neighbour of mine told me that she was interested in getting the console as a gift for her son. I told her about the offer and she was very surprised and happy and told me she'd go the next day and buy it. A few days later and once the offer was over, I met my neighbour again and asked her if her son had been happy with his present. She looked sad and told me that she didn't manage to buy it. I was surprised and asked her why not and she told me: "Like I told you, I went the next day to the department store and they had run out. I decided to go back the next day and got there before the doors opened, but there was already a long queue of people waiting. On seeing that I turned round and left. Next day I did the same thing, but I waited in the queue for a hour until finally I got tired and left. On the fourth day I did the same and went there with the same result and on the last day of the offer the same happened. In the end the offer finished and I did not manage to buy it. Worst of all, the following week I wanted to buy it in another place at full price but they had sold out and I haven't managed to buy one for my son."

This is a clear example of impatience. My neighbour didn't have the patience to wait in the queue. She did not want to have to pay the price (in this case waiting to go into the department store to buy the console), and as a result her son was very disappointed as he did not get the present he wanted.

The conclusion is that we must be patient and when the results are not as quick as we expected them, before getting impatient and making the wrong decisions we must count to ten, or twenty, or as big a number as necessary, because if we don't, instead of achieving our goal, what will happen is that we'll become frustrated, we'll get blocked and we won't be able to achieve new objectives.

There's a saying in Spanish: "La pacienciaes la madre de la ciencia" (Patience is the mother of science). That's very true. If we think about it many scientific discoveries and inventions are the result of patient researchers who did not give up as soon as things got difficult. If they had not been constant and patient, they would not have managed to complete their research projects and would not have achieved their objectives. Although there are rare discoveries that are the result of serendipity, most of them require hard work, being constant and following a well-designed plan (equivalent to the method of the realistic positive aptitude).

You will have reached the conclusion that all those people who are not naturally patient should try and make an effort to acquire the habit of patience. The best way to achieve that is to visualise the objective we are trying to achieve. Next we have to mentally visualise how we will feel when we have achieved our goal, how happy we'll be, how satisfied we will feel for having achieved our reward, and how such happy state of mind will allow us to set up new objectives and achieve new goals.

If you have reached this part of the book I can tell you that: First, you are looking for a formula to change certain things in your life. Second, you have been sufficiently constant to have read to this point. And, third, that you are patient, as otherwise you would have already closed the book.

Therefore, carry on reading. You're on the right track and the only thing you need is a little push to be successful in everything you wish to do. I hope reading this book will give you that little push.

9. The Couple

Human beings more than any other creature, experience the need to share and feel loved. Whenever we have achieved something in life, the first thing we have done is to share it with somebody. That somebody would normally be the person who occupies the first place in our hearts at that time. It might have been a friend, a relative or our couple.

Our close family, for example our parents and siblings, are a very important part of our support network, particularly when we're setting objectives throughout our lives, but in most cases they cannot be totally focused on us to help us along the way. Our parents, for example, can help us, but it they have other children too (our siblings), their effort will be divided amongst all of them.

A similar thing happens with our friends. They might love us dearly and would be ready to do anything for us, but they're in a similar to our close relatives. They also have their own parents, sibling and friends, and in many cases partners, and that means they cannot support our projects a hundred per cent, although they'll be very happy when we are successful.

But what is the position of our couple? If you think about it, socially, although they have not been born into our family, they become a part of the family. I'm sure if somebody asks you who the members of your family are, you will reply something like: "In my close family I have my parents, my sibling, my children (if you have them) and my partner."

Nobody excludes their partner (if they have one) from their familial milieu.

Some time ago, whilst I was surfing the net, I read this (I apologised to the person or persons who posted this, as I can't recall exactly its source): "Our couple is considered part of the family because s/he never gives up, is always there without expecting anything in return, offers us unforgettable and unique moments, and all because his/her love for us."

I recommend you that you don't walk alone down the path you have started by reading this book, but instead you should look for that person who will be your partner in your project and who will support you till you achieve success.

Life is like a carriage, it's easier to pull by a team of two than by a lone horse. Our current times make it even more important and necessary to have the support of our couple. Hence, our first objective to improve our circumstances should be to find that person who will help us in the difficult times, who will support us in the critical moments, who will comfort us in the moments of sadness and who will share our happiness as we reach the partial achievable realistic objectives. Take action with your partner. If you work together as if you were one, this will help you both achieve everything you wish for. Your couple is the vitamin you need every day. Your happiness and your success are in the hands of your partner.

In this book you have learned the technique of the realistic mental aptitude to achieve success, but the road to follow won't be easy. You will have hard times, when you will need somebody's support and encouragement. In those moments your "couple" will play a fundamental role. You must lean on him (or her) and to do that it's very important that they are truly involved and a part of your project, that they share your objectives and understand and apply the realistic mental aptitude.

If you make a good team with your couple and you complement each other and s/he supports you, you'll feel more self-assured and certain of your actions, you will feel loved and fulfilled, and this will make you as strong as a rock, nearly indestructible. There won't be anything capable of stopping you or making you lose your enthusiasm. Your path towards success, instead of being a harsh upward climb will become a wander around the plains. You'll see no hurdles, only your objectives well within your touch.

I'm going to tell you the story of somebody I met.

"A man once told me that he got married for the first time when he was twenty five years old. At the time he was the boss in a food company. At the same time he worked for a security firm on the weekends, and if that weren't enough, he opened his own small business selling newspapers, magazines, and some groceries. To begin with his wife was very supportive, but with

time she became tired and was no longer behind him and his projects, although she did not want to give up her lifestyle. This man was working sixteen hours per day, whilst his wife just threw away every last penny he made. Their relationship got more and more strained, and the stress of his poor relationship ended up affecting his employment. He gave up work at the food company; he also stopped working for the security firm, and his own business suffered to such point that he was obliged to sell it to avoid it major losses. Their financial situation worsened in sync with the collapse of his marriage, and finally they got divorced.

A few months later he met another woman. He was convinced he'd met his other half. Like him, she was a determined and entrepreneurial person and they opened a new business, in this case a private teaching academy. His partner had a degree in Economics and she supported him teaching. Everything went well for a few years, but then his partner decided to seek her own professional avenue. She got a job as a financial advisor for a company, she started doing the accounts for some businesses, and eventually she severed her links with the academy completely. Due to their separate jobs their relationship cooled down and became more distant. Once more the business at the academy suffered, the relationship with his couple also suffered, it eventually broke down and they went their separate ways.

This man never stopped looking for the source of his success and opened another business, this time a computer shop. To being with it was very hard, as he had no support, but after a while the business took off. He met a woman and everything seemed perfect. The business was going well and he had also found somebody who would support him and with whom he could share his success. Shortly after they got married. The first few months were perfect. One day his wife suggested that as the shop was going so well, maybe they should try and open another one. He agreed and they opened a second shop. The plan was that he would stay in one of the shops and his wife in the other one, but one good day his wife told him that he had found a job elsewhere and she was no longer going to be in charge of the second shop. This meant that he had to be in charge of both shops. The second shop started to have problems, to have losses, and what's still worse, the first one also was negatively affected, and finally he had to close down both shops. The same process followed and like in previous relationships things started to deteriorate and finally he got divorced again.

But this man had two clear objectives. The first one, being a very enterprising person, was that he would not stop until he achieved the success he was looking for. The second one was that he would achieve his success by sharing his dream with his partner.

He tried once again. He met a wonderful woman who understood him well, who supported him and offered him encouragement. Very soon he undertook new projects and this time his partner supported him throughout, she shared the moments of success, and she supported him and encouraged him when things were difficult. He eventually achieved his final objective.

This man told me that he had learned a few things: the first one, that money is important to a certain extent. The second: that you should never give up, that you must keep trying to achieve your desired objective. And third, that he would never have achieved his objective without his current wife by his side. He was fully convinced that a wonderful woman, perfect for him, existed, and it was just a matter of looking for her until he found her. If you talk to him today he'll tell you he's the happiest man in the world."

This story illustrates the importance of having a couple. If our couple offers us support and encouragement, success is sure. However, if instead of helping us and spurring us on, s/he makes our life miserable, it is likely that we will fail (and as we've seen that happened to this man with his first three partners).

Happiness is our natural state. It's like a plant with many branches. We must water it every day to bring it to bloom. Water your happiness every day and in the place of compost add the love for your couple and you'll see how it flowers much quicker.

When researching this topic I've found that in the great majority of cases behind each person who succeeds, there's another offering support and encouragement.

It makes me think of a great Spanish painter who used to say: "My muse, the source of my inspiration, is my wife".

When we are emotionally stable with our couple, we can achieve any goals, we feel able to be successful at anything we try.

It is of vital importance that we share with our couple the efforts and hardships, the happy moments and the successes we reach.

I'm sure that if you don't have a couple at the moment you'll be wondering: Does all of this mean that because I don't have a couple, even if I apply this book's technique I will never reach my goals? Of course you can be successful in whatever you try. The point of this chapter is to make people realise that all those who have partners and are planning on using the realistic mental aptitude, should get them involved in the project, make sure that they share in the setting of objectives, and by doing so they will support each other mutually and the road to success will be smooth.

If we have a partner s/he must add value to our objectives, not subtract or create hurdles. It's very difficult to achieve success with a dead weight around your neck that prevents you from reaching it.

The conclusion is simple. If you don't have a couple that is not a problem. You can start on the road towards your objectives by yourself, with your own strength, but if you have a couple, it's important that they become involved in everything are doing or are going to do. They should not be an extra load slowing you down, they should be your support, your trampoline.

10. What are the obstacles preventing you from becoming successful?

Until now you have followed a path, you have read how to adopt a realistic mental aptitude, how to develop it, which are the important points to take into account…If you have read the book to this point, there must be a reason. If you have only read it but have not applied any of the theories I have explained, or completed the exercises in previous chapters, my question is: What is preventing you from achieving success in everything you wish? Why haven't you started putting the theory into practice?

I'll tell you a story to make the point clearer.

"Many years ago there was a granddad who had two birds, to be more specific he had two gorgeous budgies. He had them since they were born. He kept them in a big cage, shiny, clean, with little swings for them to play, feeders and even some toys to keep them happy and entertained. The granddad was quite old and as was to be expected he died one day and when his relatives went to his house to collect his belongings they saw the cage with the two budgies.

One of the relatives asked what they were going to do with them, who was going to take them home. Nobody replied. Nobody was prepared to have them at home and have to worry about looking after them in the way granddad had been doing till then. In that moment of doubt one of the relatives suggested the idea of opening the cage and setting them free. After some discussion all present agreed to do that. Then, a ten years old girl, the granddaughter of the man, crying and very sad opened the cage and said: “Budgies you’re free to start a new life. You’re free forever.”

At the beginning, the budgies looked towards the open door but didn’t move. Several hours went by and they carried on playing in the cage and eating, until one of them landed on the open door, looked first to one side and then to the other, and finally flew away, first around the cage a few times and eventually flew out through an open window.

The other little bird was left alone, sad, looking around the cage, missing something. He no longer had the granddad talking to him or his partner playing with him in the cage.

Every day the relatives went to the house to sort paperwork out, until they finished their entire task and stopped going. A few days later they went to granddad's apartment and saw that the budgie had died. It had died of sadness and starvation, with the door open as they had left it. And by the window was the other budgie flying around."

Do you know what had happened? Very simple. One of the budgies had decided to try a different path, to explore new horizons, to seek new opportunities, whilst the other one stayed in the cage and did nothing. But its life was no longer the same, as it was alone, and vulnerable, but the familiarity and comfort with the situation stopped him from leaving the cage.

There might have been a number of reasons why it would not seek new roads and leave: the comfortable situation it had lived in until that moment, because it was the only life it'd ever known, or because it didn't' want to fight to get to know a different way of life.

I want you to think about that. If you acquire a realistic mental aptitude with the technique you've learned in this book and you plan a different life for yourself, with achievable objectives, you are constant and you follow all the steps we have looked at in previous chapters, what prevents you from achieving success? Being comfortable with your situation can't be the reason, because if you're reading this book that means you're looking for a change. I don't think being afraid of the unknown would be the reason either. If you are in a very difficult situation, what would you be afraid of? Improving your lot? It could be because you don't have the required means or resources. But I don't think that's a valid reason either. As we have seen you just need to adapt to the current circumstances, move forward slowly, achieving partial realistic objectives that will allow you to reach the final objectives in time.

If that's the case, what is preventing you from reaching your goals? What is impeding your change? What is blocking your attempts at taking a new path?

You don't know, do you? Let's have look at another story that might clarify matters:

"In a book that listed curious facts about animals I read that the imperial eagle is one of the animals that can live the longest, up to seventy

years. It's a bird of prey. It lives of hunting, it's a predatory bird, and it has a strong beak and sharp claws that allow it to hunt surprisingly heavy preys in comparison to its own weight.

When they reach approximately the middle point of their lives (thirty something years), their beak and claws weaken, and that can cause them serious problems with their hunting and therefore their survival.

What the imperial eagle does when it reaches this point is to feed as much as it can, gain strength for a long journey, and with the energy it has accumulated it travels to a high peak far away from its usual habitat.

Once it reaches its destination, it begins to hit its beak with tremendous force on the floor, rocks, until it manages to wrench the beak, and it does the same with its claws. It hits them mercilessly until they break and fall off.

A few days later, without food, but with enough fat reserves to survive, its beak and claws start growing again, and eventually they reach a similar consistency and strength as they had before, when they were young. When this moment arrives and with the limited energy they have left, they start their journey back again to their territory, with the new beak and claws, and they start to hunt and eat, dominating again the horizon with their long and graceful wings, powerful beak and razor-sharp claws. In this way they survive until they die of old age”

It’s an impressive story and an example of the realistic mental aptitude we need if we are not in the right situation or in the best conditions to achieve our objectives. To start on our new path we must break with anything that stands on our way. We must learn from the imperial eagle and get rid of anything that prevents us from achieving success.

Change everything that oppresses you, everything that holds you back, everything that is negative and does not allow you to be successful.

We mustn’t be afraid of becoming successful, we must not do like the budgie in the cage.We should not be afraid of suffering to achieve our objective.You know you can do it, you only need to think and find out what’s holding you back and break the ties that prevent you from being the best you can be. Break away from those ties and start the path with a strong will, illusion, strength and faith in yourself.

Success is within your reach, fly, tear anything that holds you back, adopt a realistic mental aptitude, follow all the steps of the technique described in this book, and without fear you'll achieve what you want so much. You must not be afraid of success, you should only be frightened of doing nothing and letting things carry on as they are.

11. The Game of Your Life

We have heard it said many times that life is like a game. And it's true; life is a game we must play, but how? What are the rules?

I think life is like a chess game. Don't be worried although I'm sure some of you might not like or know how to play the game. I don't intend for you to learn how to play, but I just want to make a comparison between a chess game and our life.

I am going to give you a brief definition of a chess game.

“Chess is a rational game, with two players. Each one of them has eight pairs of pawns, a pair of rooks, a pair of horses, a pair of bishops, a king with its queen, all placed within a chessboard made up of seventy four squares. The chess pieces are either black or white. The player with the white pieces starts the game and makes the first move and then it’s the turn of the player who has the black ones, and they alternate moving their pieces.

There are so many possible moves for each player that it is impossible to calculate all the possible combinations.

The objective of the player it to win the game by defeating his opponent, achieving what is called a check-mate, but as the game develops it is necessary to obtain advantageous positions, and winning moves, and sometimes to do so we must sacrifice one of our pieces.

The winner is the one who places the other player's pieces in check-mate."

I will explain how a game of chess might serve as comparison with our life.

Our chessboard is everything that surrounds us; the place where we live, the people around us, our family, our friends, etc.

When we are born we are like the player with the white pieces who is the one to start the game.The black pieces are life, specifically everything that happens around us and to us.

Our pieces are the tools we have to play throughout our life.

Every time we make a move in our life, another move takes place. Sometimes it might be exactly the one we wanted and it suits us well, but sometimes it might go against us.

Our partial realistic objective is to reach advantageous moves and positions that will allow us to achieve our final realistic objective, to win the game, in the end.

Sometimes in our lives we make moves that are not the best, and the same happens when we play chess. What we must do at that time is to rectify as we have seen in previous chapters. In many occasions we might need to sacrifice a piece or two to obtain a more advantageous position (you will remember some of the examples we have discussed in the book, for example when my friends, who trained as nurses, had to sacrifice staying at home with their families to achieve their dreams).

When we have made all the correct moves, we win the game, we do check-mate, we are successful and we win the game of our own life.

That means you must play the game of your life, be rational, adopt a realistic mental aptitude, change your moves in accordance to the moves that life makes around you, rectify if you realise you are not achieving you goals, consider making sacrifices if it is necessary to achieve your objective. You must always move your pieces according to a strategy. Winning the game of your life only depends on you.

Like in a game of chess, you are the only one who can play the game of your life; nobody can play it for you. Sometimes that's the mistake we make, we want others to play for us. You can accept advice from the people around you, but you'll soon realise that success only depends on you and your aptitude.

I'm sure you will have noticed sometimes that when things are going well, we are in a happy relationship, our family life is good and our financial position is sound, we have plenty of people around us. However, when things start to go wrong and we're at our worst, how many people stay with us and remain supportive? How it is that everybody disappears?

For that reason I want you to be aware that you're the only one with the answer to your problems, and it's in your hands. You're the only one who can play the game of your life and reach check-mate, success.

Don't let negative people bring you down, don't allow anybody to put hurdles on your game, don't listen to anybody who tells you that you can't win. Why? Because your success or failure depends on how you play the game.

In this book you have learned a technique that allows you to play the game of your life, make use of it. These are easy steps, in a sequence, but however simple it is up to you to take them. Nobody else will move the pieces in the game of your life for you. You must be the player. And it is no good either to refuse to play. You were born and that put you on the chessboard, you must play; it's up to you if you win or lose the game.

Play with your head, with a realistic outlook, rationally, with confidence, with patience, be constant, rectify when it's necessary, but most of all set yourself one objective TO WIN THE GAME OF YOUR LIFE, TO ACHIEVE SUCCESS.

12 Start Walking Down Your Path

The mental realistic aptitude is the technique that will help you start on the path to success.

Many people who are successful, who have achieved fame and fortune, have applied the technique. Without even being aware of it they have applied each and every one of the steps that I have described in the book. You only have to think about somebody you know who has been successful on some field or other, and reflect about how they achieved their success, and you'll be surprised to notice that indeed they followed the steps we've studied without having the book in their hands.

This is the key. I have read many books talking about successful people, and analysing their methods and achievements I came up with the technique I've shared with you.

In the book's prologue I highlighted how this theory will allow you to obtain any objective you decide on, and that's the case. I will suggest some examples of situations and objectives where you could use the technique to achieve your goal.

"If you are looking for a job, use this technique. You need to be realistic as the current situation is difficult, but you must set yourself partial realistic objectives, study the options you have, use all the tools you have at your hands (distribute CVs every day, talk to people offering yourself for work, etc.), take action, be constant and don't lose faith, be patient, rectify if you see that you're not achieving your objectives, and if you follow these steps I'm sure you'll get a job."

"You can also use this technique to find your ideal partner, the couple you dream of every day. You must use the technique, but it's important to remember to have a realistic mental aptitude. We cannot enamour somebody who is beyond our reach, you must set yourself a realistic objective, and you must use all the tools available. Get to know everything possible about the person, their likes and dislikes, and make them realise that you are their ideal couple.Be constant in your pursuit; rectify if you make mistakes, and if you have to sacrifice something for that person, do it, and pay the price for success."

You can apply this technique to any objectives of your life, no matter if they are personal or material.

Another important aspect of the technique is that you can apply it as many times as you like and as you achieve successes you will become more confident and assured in your realistic mental aptitude.

Start on your path to success. Do this exercise: choose a partial realistic objective, check what the tools at your disposal are, take action and be constant. If you see that instead of getting closer to your objective you are getting further and further, you must rectify, and as we've seen, you have to be prepared to pay the price for success.

In the prologue and throughout the book I have told you in several occasions to write down all the exercises I suggested. At the end of the book you have three empty pages to do the exercises. Now, I'm going to give you my last piece of advice. In a sheet of paper write down an achievable partial realistic objective, analyse the tools you have within your reach to achieve it, write down the steps you need to follow (take action, be constant, rectify if necessary and pay the price). As you carry on the steps, you can tick those you have already applied, and that way you can see your progress, and in the end you'll realise you have achieved your objective.

It's very important that you complete this step. Sometimes if we have not written down what we want to achieve or do, we cannot be sure of exactly where we are. You need to always know what you want and how you're doing. For you this piece of paper will be like a guide. It will also be useful to remind you what end you're working towards, what is your final achievable realistic objective.

Do you think a building or a house can be built without blueprints? I'm sure you've seen on more than one occasion architects, draughtsmen, builders, etc., in a building site. They're always walking around with papers in their hands. These papers are usually the blueprints of the building they're working on. They use them as a guide and without them they could not complete the building. You must do the same. You must have the blueprints of what you want to achieve, you

also need to know what tools you have at your disposal and must be aware of how you are progressing through the different steps of the realistic mental aptitude.

Go on; take pen and paper and start writing or designing the blueprints of the road to your success.

You've learned the technique in this book, you know what you want, and you need to do it.

If you have arrived this far, I want to congratulate you because you have started down **THE PATH TO SUCCESS.**

FLOWCHART

Realistic Mental Aptitude
Setting partial realistic objectives
Setting final realistic objective
Take action
Be constant
Rectify
Pay the price
SUCCESS

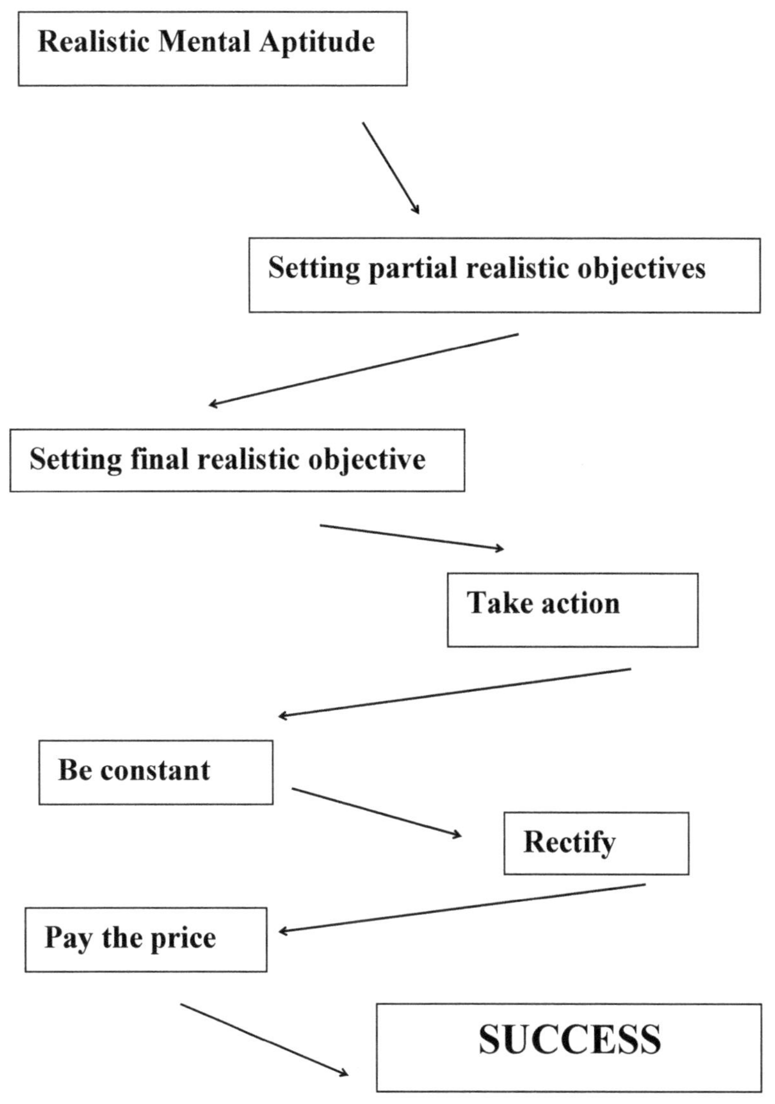

Notes

Other books by the autor

Friendships and Betrayals:

Synopsis: 'Friendships and Betrayals' is a fictional story based on reality. Saverio, the protagonist tells us about his experience of the last five years. He has a computer repair shop but his friend Vicent convinces him to go to work to the Princess Hospital, where he has been working for the last thirty years. There he meets a lot of people, he makes friends and he even marries one of his female colleagues. But in the end these friends and colleagues betray him, and he ends up in a very complicated and nasty situation. During his time working at the hospital he witnesses situations and facts he would never have imagined, envy, corruption, procrastination, undue use of influences to employ friends and relatives, opportunism, thefts, fraud, and a great variety of unexpected experiences.

Link to the novel:

https://www.facebook.com/AmistadesYTraiciones

Link to the Facebook page for the book 'The Realistic Mental Aptitude, the Solution to Your Problems':

https://www.facebook.com/LaAptitudMentalRealista

Author's webpage:

http://javieralmenar.jimdo.com/

www.ingramcontent.com/pod-product-compliance
Ingram Content Group UK Ltd.
Pitfield, Milton Keynes, MK11 3LW, UK
UKHW020128250726
13967UKWH00002B/537